Praises
in
Phrases

Soon The Second Coming
(Time is Short)

ANDREW HECTOR

Paperback: 978-1-965632-00-0
eBook: 978-1-965632-01-7
Library of Congress Control Number: 2024918716

Ordering Information:

Prime Seven Media
518 Landmann St.
Tomah City, WI 54660

Printed in the United States of America

To the Father,
Son,
and
Holy Spirit.
(Preparing the way for the Lord.)

TABLE OF CONTENTS

PREFACE

*I*f you are a believer or a non-believer that is your choice. Since the time of Adam and Eve, God has given us free will-the freedom to choose which path to take in our lives.

The Lord has asked me to publish these poems. He didn't order me, He gave me the choice. He left it up to my free will. These writings came to me in Psalms, as Psalms came to David in the Bible.

When I was in grade 4 at school, I was hit on the head with a broken roof tile and died for one and half minutes. I elevated high above and looked down on the three- or four-storey building which looked the size of a cigarette box. I remember smiling down on the group of school children with love. Ever since then, I have been aware of the afterlife.

Certain things have happened between the Lord and me since then. When I was approximately twenty-five, nail prints in the shape of the capital 'I' appeared on both my wrists. The pain cut to the bone through my wrists and lasted for ten days and nights. Now whether the enemy did this to me or not is debatable as, at that stage, I was naive to his ways. This happened after I had been rejected by someone I loved. I remember during the time of the nail prints, the Lord had said to me that He had been rejected too.

I first became aware of the enemy just prior to Tiananmen Square 1989. I was living in Adelaide during my first spiritual war at this time.

It was during this time that I first battled against the enemy and served the Lord in a very special way. I have been in many battles against the enemy in the name of the Lord since that time. I am only telling you this personal story to try and give credence to what I am about to say.

The poetry I have written was inspired by the Heavenly Father and the Lord Jesus Christ. You will notice that the majority of the poems were written in the early hours of the morning. I would be asleep, and the first two lines of the poem would constantly repeat themselves. The only way I could sleep was to write them down.

As soon as I wrote them down, the next lines would come immediately to mind, and so I would write them down straight away, hence the times beside my poems. You must believe that I would not sit there for hours and work out what to say. You must also believe that I didn't sit and write for the sake of it.

I only wrote these poems when it was the Lord's will, hence the gap of two years since the last few poems. The reason for this was that I was waiting for directions from the Lord as to what to do about these poems. I knew that, eventually, the time would come when he would direct me to his cause.

The Lord has shown me over the years that this is a battle of logistics and tactics as if you were playing chess. It is important for the Lord that the enemy is uncertain about what is to happen next. I am no fool. I know that in the past, people have prophesised that the Lord would come back during their time. However, looking at the poems sent to me, it is exciting to believe that the Lord will be back in my lifetime.

On the other hand, if He doesn't, I will not be surprised either. The Lord works in mysterious ways. I remember in one of my poems, He says, 'I will catch you later.' Well, this could be either in life or in death. In the 'Wedding Ring' poem, this could be either in my lifetime or in the future.

The important thing is you must believe the main message behind this poetry that the Lord Jesus Christ is real. He is coming back. *He is coming back soon.*

So please, if you are a non-believer, please consider reading the Bible and turn to the Lord, for He will direct you and save you. If you have sinned as I have, it makes no matter. The Lord would say to you, 'I forgive you for your sins. I do not remember them. Now go your way and sin no more.'

I conclude by saying I have faith in the Lord and believe the time is now ripe for His return. Consider how crowded Earth is with its billions of people and the fact that we are now venturing outside this planet and polluting His universe. Yes, the enemy is within all of us. This is a fact. We have the sin of death in us. It is like a blood poisoning which has been passed down the bloodline since the time of Adam and Eve.

Only the Lord can cure us of this, and this will happen when He returns, when His allotted time comes. This time is coming, and it will happen *soon.*

Looking forward to His return,
Andrew Hector

YOUR KINGDOM COME

3:30–4:00 a.m., 18 April 1994

You Mystify me. You are glorious to me.
I sing songs of praises to You.
You come to me when all is quiet.
You colour my world. I love You so.

Hence, when You come to me,
I kneel before You, my Lord.
I am like an anxious bride
Thirsting for my master.

I thirst for You, my Lord.
Oh, how I long to see Your return.

We have been cocooned in eons of darkness.
I can see Your rising LIGHT on the horizon of darkness.
The embryo sees the light and longs for the birth.
Man will be reborn.

We are evolving to be glorified by You.
We seek to reclaim that which was lost
As Your paradise returns to Your children.
We Glorify You.
We sing songs of never-ending praise to You.
We worship You.
We love You so.
Jesus, I long to see Your Kingdom come.

For so too as You Glorify us,
We will Glorify You.
We will have much to do for You
As Your Universe unfolds as it should.

THE STAR

2:00–2:30 p.m., 18 April 94

Jesus, my Lord, You entered
my heart, carrying Your
shepherd's staff.

You are my guide, my defender,
My guard, my bastion.
You stand firm, unflinching
With strength or purpose.

You are my friend,
You are my rock.
I am Your friend,
I am Your rock.

You are my Saviour.
I love You so.
Our evil enemy of darkness will be defeated.
His tool of death will become succulent
To himself, his only friend.

As death is defeated and Your enemies
become Your footstool, You will be glorified.

The whole Universe will see the light of Your glory
And the Earth as the hub
In the spokes of Your wheel.

And God's creation will have erupted
With sparks of energy,
And Your Universe will know man –
The Son of Man.

Your Kingdom come.
Your will be done.

MUDDY WATERS

4:00 p.m., 18 April 1994

You are the waterfall,
And I am the water jug.
You are the source,
And I am the container.

As the water spills out,
You are my inspiration.
Let the water flow,
And the ice will melt.

Let the rocks purify the water so that
The mud becomes the container!
A transformation Glory days. Hallelujah!

And many vessels will be born,
Carrying the pure water.
Glory days. Hallelujah!

THE ORCHARD

9:30 a.m., 19 April 1994

I am a tree in Your orchard.
So that I can be the fruit of Your vine,
Cut the rotten fruit from my branches.

I look up at the beaming rays of Your rainbow
And see a dove take flight,
Descending on a path to my tree.
It sits on my branches.

Oh, to be like this dove,
Pure and white,
At peace in flight,
You are my chosen one.

What's this I see?
A city of gold descends on me.
Its walls a splendour
With rays of light.

And I see my friend the dove.
It takes flight and lands
On all the trees in the orchard.
The orchard shrieks with delight
As all the rotting fruit drops from its branches.

Oh, what a beautiful crop we show
Perfect in every way.
Our leaves spring out and glow.
Like that dove, we are.
'Thank you,' we say.

And the groom looked upon the bride
And said, 'In you, I am well pleased.
You are the dove at My side'.
And through the orchard came the breeze!

THE DOVE

3:00 a.m., 20 April 1994

You are the dove.
I watch you in peaceful flight.
In you, there is love.
In you, there is peace at night.

You fly on a straight and narrow course
Surrounded by birds of prey.
Nothing can touch you, of course.
You are a symbol for what we pray.

THE HORSE

9:30 a.m., 2 May 1994

You are My horse.
You are My warrior, My fighter,
My stallion.

You stand firm in the face of danger,
Unflinching, My companion.

Your faith in Me is immeasurable.
Your trust in Me is deep.
Together, we face the wrath of our enemy,
With one purpose in mind –
His defeat.

Together, we faced the eons of darkness.
We rode into the valley of death.
I nurtured you through the danger.
I held you with My soothing caress.

We travelled the void together.
We returned to our homeland.
We came back to paradise.

And now our journey is ending.
And now our goal is in sight.
We are reclaiming our birthright.
We are reclaiming our paradise.

And Heaven will come to Earth.
And our two domains will be as one,
And dimensional travel is a concept–
A concept that will be proved to be won!

PUPPETS ON A STRING

5:30 a.m., 20 June 1994

There is a man who walks the streets.
His heart is slow to the beat.
His mind, body, and spirit are one.
The play has been undone.

For we are all just puppets on a string,
Don't fight this wonderful thing,
For we all have one purpose in mind –
To be all, one of a kind.

Our aim is to please Our Lord, Our King,
Our Father, Our God!
Their aim is to please Their Family, Their Ring,
His Bride, His Children, His Rod!

He created us in His image.
Oh, how we long to see His face.
He has planned a family of full lineage
To reclaim this Earth; after all, it is His Place.

QUANTUM LEAP

12:10–12:40 a.m., 22 June 1994

Giant steps are what you get
By walking on the moon
And when Jesus comes back with no regret,
Which is none too soon.

For what He wants
Is to test this shrill,
This Family of Man.

There will be the best and less
Put to the test.
Be with Him if you can.

A Quantum Leap
Is what we'll reap,
His Family of Man.

God's Universe beckons us
To sow His seed
And to spread out
As a fan.

For Heaven and Earth Will be as one,
The Hub of His wheel.
And the Father and Son
Will walk this place.
Oh, what a thrill.

For Peace and Tranquillity
Will be known by Man
And the Universe
As a whole.

And the Father and Son
And ALL THEIR SAINTS
Will be as our cup and bowl.

For our spiritual birth
Comes to Earth,
For it is Mother Earth's role.

To ENVELOPE God's Children and His Son,
So that OUR SPIRIT CAN BE AS ONE
AND IN FULL CONTROL.

THE TAP

3:30 a.m., 24 June 1994

Tap! Tap! Tappety Tap!
Who's that?
It is I, your Lord.
I want you to be My sword.

For I am Your inspiration.
You're My instigation,
My tool,
My warrior,
My word!

I tap you on the shoulder.
I'll make you even bolder,
For I am your source
Your water!

I plan your course.
My Fighter! My Soldier!
I am the tap,
The source, the switch,
On and off at My command,
Not a problem, without a hitch,
Not even a glitch.

My little prize fighter,
My warrior, My word,
I'll catch you later
As you'll see FREEDOM come to MY world.

For I AM
The BRIGHT MORNING STAR,
The ALPHA and OMEGA.
I have come from afar
To be both your KING and LEADER.

7:30 a.m., 24 July 1994

I have come in the Spirit.
Keep searching the skies.
Yes, I am coming soon from afar,
And you'll know the word.
SURPRISE! SURPRISE! SURPRISE!

A CODE IN THE NIGHT

2:00 a.m., 25 June 1994

I am Within.
I am Without.
I am from all about.

I am Jesus.
I am your Lord.
When I come,
I'll be yelling,
'All Aboard!'

I have put you on a path of discovery,
I'll lead you to a full recovery,
I'll take you to My shining light,
And everything will be completely and fully all right.

I am your beacon in the night.
Come to Me if you like.
Overcome your enemy of fear and fright,
And I will show you a smile and pure delight.

I am tapping out My code to you in the night,
Awaiting your response with eager delight,
For the next verse will be from you, not Me, all right.
Our readers must be enjoying this out of sight!

You are my lighthouse in the night,
A beam of light shining bright,
Shining Your light so that I can see.
Through this veil of darkness, You will come to me.

You shine Your light so that I can see.
I was once blind and now I see.
You have dispensed with my darkness and enemy.
And, as night becomes day, given me clarity.

Lord, I love You.
I am in Your fold.
You have given me warmth
And brought me in from the cold.

For YOU ARE MY HOLY TRINITY,
MY INFINITY, MY GOLD.
You shower me with Your Spirit
And fill my cup, my bowl.

No love compares with Yours.
No giving so deep,
I would like to write no end in praise for You,
But for now I must sleep.

MARCH OF JESUS

9:15 a.m., 25 June 1994

It is our inalienable right
Stated at birth.
It is our fate by origin
To reclaim this Earth.

Today we show our faith in the Trinity
Who sowed the seed.
We march for humanity.
Oh, how we bleed.

He looks down on us
With sad and loving eyes
On a planet torn by corruption,
Polluted by evil and lies.

As we band ourselves together
And our world of tribes become as one,
We know it is just a matter of time
Before we see Jesus come.

Our Lord, God's only Son,
Our KING, our EMPEROR, our SWORD,
Our DRAGON SLAYER, KING OF KINGS,
LORD of LORDS,
OUR MOST HOLY ONE.

For it is His will,
It is His statement, His goal,
To bring freedom to His people
And to fulfil His role.

He will turn to mankind and say,
'Who are My people? It is your will!
For My arms are outstretched,
My shoulders are broad and still.'

'I will take all those who want Me.
No hypocrites or liars,
Only those who stand by Me.
To loyalty, I aspire.'

'And I will take you on a giant step
Of spiritual awareness by birth,
For you are ALL about to be born,
And the UNIVERSE WILL KNOW THIS EARTH.'

AMEN.

GLORY BOUND TO GOD

3:30 a.m., 27 June 1994

God, You turn us into saints,
Lift us to higher ground,
Show us ALL Your mercy.
To You, we are glory bound.

You take us on a journey,
Put us in good stead,
Feed us milk and honey,
Give us peace and bread.

You are our mighty Creator.
To You, we owe our life.
You sent Your Son to save us,
Your Lamb as a sacrifice.

For He came to teach us a valuable lesson
And defeat the enemy at hand.
It was on the hill of Calvary
Where Jesus made His stand.

He was heavenly sent from above
To teach us all a lesson
Through His death and resurrection –
The ULTIMATE ACT OF LOVE.

The angels are ascending and descending,
Two dimensions transcending.
The endplay we now enhance.
The trumpets and cymbals pronounce.

For the coming of Jesus Christ is near.
His Spirit is ALREADY HERE.
He has let me know I am His scout,
And there are many of us about.

Peace, Harmony, and Tranquillity we will know.
To the Universe, our spiritual birth we will show
As we triumph over death and all its ills.
That day is coming that JESUS instils.

MY HORSE

3:30 a.m., 29 June 1994

My Horse, my Horse,
You take me on a course
To mountains of beauty
And desire.

Up the track,
Beauty front and back,
You lift me
Higher and higher.

You take me to the peak.
Words I cannot speak
As my eyes lie to rest
On the rainforest, mountains,
Valleys, and ocean crest.

A partnership we have had,
You have made me so glad
To rest easy on your back,
On your strength,
Your hooves in clay.

Through eons of time,
You have carried me.
Into battles you have taken me
And on peaceful rides to this day.

Your loyalty I admire.
Space and freedom we desire.
A bond that will always stay
Forever and a day.

LONELINESS

3:15–4:00 a.m., 9 July 1994

It is a time of despair
When there is no one there
Of solitude
An interlude.

A time of trial
Of self-reflection
Like a bile
One seeks self-protection.

A time of faith
A time of hope
A seeking path
Throw me that safety rope.

A time of tribulation
A time of fear
A time to face your enemy
Without friends so dear.

A time of rejection
And of self-pity
A natural reaction
My tears fall, overlooking that city.

A time of disappointment
That was my appointment
To be abandoned by all other
Not one could help me,
Not even my Father.

A time of self-confidence
A time to make a stand
This is my incidence.
There must be a lesson at hand.

A time to overcome all fear
To break from captivity
To put yourself into gear
And learn creativity.

A time to reach out to others
And show what you can give
Rise up, sister and brother,
And learn how to live.

A time of solitude and confinement
When no one comprehends you
A time of refinement
When one tastes the morning dew.

This was our gift to Jesus.
When He was nailed to the cross,
He destroyed the destroyer
And all the diseases.
That was His gift to us.

As you give out, God rewards you.
He seated His Son
At His right hand.
That was His due.
His precious begotten one
Hand in hand
Oh, they look so grand
Seated as ONE.

Loneliness for us to see Them
Oh, how They long for us to know freedom
To be with us
To UNIFY us
To BE AS ONE.

To WIN THE RACE
To LIVE IN THIS PLACE
Face to face with HIS SON.
Praise the Lord.

PAIN

It cuts to the bone.
It belongs to the enemy's throne.
Like a dartboard
Numbered with names,
He throws at will.
His ultimate aim
Is to kill.

That ultimate act of despair,
He throws suicide in the air.
He loves to scare
And knows not that word – fair.

Suicide if you dare.
He beckons you to his lair.
I say, 'Why give him the pleasure?
Let's live forever.'

PSYCH WARD

5:30–7:00 a.m., 10 July 1994

I remember that day so clearly
When they let me out of that psychiatric ward.
I was stress bound, broken down
In a spiritual war.

For three days, it was raining.
I was holding my cross.
My hands are burning.
If the enemy wins, it's my loss.

On the wall, I could see
A poster of three guys on top of a mountain.
They were looking down on me,
Saying the Lord will be my fountain.

I was surrounded by people
With that peculiar stare.
Nurses were busy working.
There was something in the air.

It started with the guy beside me.
He vomited up green.
His eyes changed, and he could see
Sights unseen.

He stopped his slurring,
His staggering,
His bad wording,
His vomiting.
You could see him thinking.

'I have been possessed.
I must have rid that demon.
I have found myself and redressed.
Oh, how I feel a clean man.'

And the dominoes started to fall
As everybody started to change.
The nurses gave the doctors a call.
'There is something being rearranged.'

And you could hear the staff muttering,
'What's going on? What's happening?

I don't know.
It is out of our control
Who stole the show?'
As they watched their patients
Start their stroll.

As they watched their patients stare,
Looks turned from a stare to a glare
Till there was nothing there.
They had been transformed
And were back to the norm.

The nurses looked agog.
They said they had never seen
Their ward change so rapidly.
It must have been heavenly
Sent from God
As they watched their patients
Walking around so happily.

Suddenly, it stopped raining,
And we all started grinning.
They let us out to play tennis.
But frankly, we couldn't care less.

It was the air we wanted,
That taste of freedom
To see the sky that building had squandered.
This feeling was like a food you could feed on.

And I looked up over the roof,
And without a word of a lie,
I could see there as plain proof
Flying evenly through the sky.

Wonders will never cease.
Sent from heaven above
A symbol of peace–
A pure white fantail dove.

It flew on a course that was straight and narrow,
Surrounded by two birds of prey.
It flew as if its destiny was not for tomorrow
But for this very day.

It never changed its course,
Untouched by its enemy,
Unhurried in flight.
God in heaven was its source.
It was a message to me.
Oh, what a sight
Of pure delight.

For I am the messenger to set you free.
Just turn to the Lord,
And He will rid that demon
That belongs to that ward –
PSYCHIATRY.

'Pray and believe in Me,
And I will meet you all the way.
Have strength and faith and turn to Me.
If you believe in Me,' the Lord would say,
'I will rid that demon
That belongs to that title
PSYCHIATRY.'

And I will return to you your personality
That comes under that title rationality,
With your own spices of character,
Your own salt and pepper,
Your own special seasoning,
Your own sauces of pleasure,
Your own special reasoning –
Everything in the right and proper measure.

You are My own special ingredient,
My child, My humble servant.
You are a part of My order.
By nature, you are obedient
As you are a part of My formula.

I AM

I am you.
I am Me.
I am in you.
Can't you see?
I am the three
Most important letters in the alphabet.
Individually, you must agree.

I am free.
I am a statement.
I am here.
I am you.
I am Me.

God's light shines in you
And shines in me.
We are all the fruit of His vine.
Can't you see?

Jesus says, 'I AM,'
As you say, 'I AM.'
It is a statement of truth,
Not a lie.
Our hands reach to the roof.
Our eyes search the sky.
When you sing to a friend

'I am going soon', it is not a lie.
For as you see Me go and ascend,
I will return and descend.
I am coming soon. I do not lie.
I am Me.
I am coming soon to set you free.

Individually, you are most important.
You say those three letters.
You are you.
And I am Me.
Be creative
Be free.

You say those three letters
'I AM'. Can't you see?
It is the truth, not a scam –
Those three letters

'I AM'.

3:40 a.m., 21 July 1994

You see ME in the Spirit.
I love every minute.
Soon you'll see ME with your eyes,
And you'll know that word.
Surprise! Surprise! Surprise!

Yes, I am coming soon.
I do not lie.
As sure as Earth has a Moon.
Keep looking to the sky.

A PROMISE

1:00–2:00 a.m., 21 July 1994

Lord, You descend
With Your saints and angels
And apostles behind.
Trumpets ablaring,
Tearing up the sky.

Your arms outstretched,
Your eyes open wide,
Your ear-to-ear grin,
Through You, we abide.

I long to see You,
To hear Your voice,
To be saved by You,
Transformed by You.
Through You, I'll rejoice.

To turn this death planet
Into a living planet –
A miracle at hand.
To see You save Your people
And cure Your oceans and land.

I long to see You tearing up the skies
Your trumpets blazing,
Fire in Your eyes,

Your arms outstretched,
Your radiant glow,
Thunder bolts and lightning,
And, of course, God's promise –
All the colours of the rainbow.

Your saints and apostles
Your angels at Your side.
You will say to us,
'Would you like to be like them?
Beauty exemplified.'

Throw down your weapons
And do as I say,
And peace, love, joy, and harmony
Will come to you this very day.

For I am the Lord,
God's only begotten Son.
I have come to save you.
I am your MOST HOLY ONE.

And I am going to take you on a journey
Of peace and tranquillity of man.
Just do as I say,
And I'll show you I can.

For eons, We have waited.
Our destiny is at hand.
God's plan is unfolding.

Oh, it looks spectacular.
It looks beautiful.
Oh, it looks so grand.
So many beautiful surprises
So many plans instore
So many gifts So many prizes.
So many voices rejoicing.
A festival of fireworks
And parties galore.

And I will set up My throne,
My most Holy home,
And I will set about putting
My house into order –
God's house, My Father's house.
He has promised this to Me –
MY HOUSE, MY HOME.

Oh, Jesus,
I long to hear You say these words.
My Lord, I bow my head before You,
My knees to the ground,
My arms outstretched.

I lay myself before You.
I humbly kiss Your ground.
Oh, Lord, I long to serve You,
To learn from You,
To hear You,
To see You.

You constantly surprise me.

You astound me.

You thrill me. Through You, this Earth will see

BEAUTY ABOUND.

Oh, if I could be so fortunate,

I would like to touch You, to shake Your hand,

And say, 'Thank You, my Lord Jesus, my King.

Thank You for saving us.

Thank You for saving me.

Thank You for saving the oceans and this land.'

AMEN.

CALVARY

1:00–3:00 a.m., 25 July 1994

Father, here I am, alone,
With nothing to lean on.
Son, outstretch Your hands
And turn to that rock, that stone.

Come rest on Me.
You are not alone.
Let Me be that rock, that stone.
On Me, You can lean on.

Oh, My burden is heavy.
Tears of blood form at My brow.
Oh, I must find strength and be steady.
These sins of the world.
Oh, they taste so foul.

I hear people coming.
My men are asleep.
Their spirit is willing.
But their flesh, it is weak.

They have taken Me away
Amidst pushing and shoving.
Oh, if only they knew our enemy,
They could be so loving.

They know not what they do.
This very day,
I have been arrested through who?
'Judas,' you say.

They have crowned Me with thorns.
They have pierced My head, My skin.
I should look at them with scorn,
But I can only feel pity within.

My precious blood has matted My head hair
And runs down My face.
It has trickled through My beard hair
And entered My lips,
On My tongue – that most sacred of taste.

The authorities throw Me around.
The high priests just stare.
I hear them say,
'Leave it to the people. It's their ground.
Let them decide.
Let them have their say.
That sounds fair.'

And they gave Me My heavy cross
To drag through the streets.
My spirit is strong,
But My burden is heavy.
And My flesh, it is weak.

A man came from the crowd
And offered to carry My cross.
He looked so proud,
His eyes loving and moist.

To lighten My load, To lighten My burden,
To share My road,
He knew that I was hurtin'.

So here we are on this hill
Overlooking My city –
A city that knows how to kill
And has no sense of pity.

Feel privileged to accompany Me
Side by side.
You two make us three.

Trust and have faith in Me.
In My Father, I abide,
And He will reward thee.

'Oh, Father, My precious blood,
It spills from My body.
These special years,

These special tears,
I cry with My special tears of blood
Overlooking this city.'

'My Son, You are My grain,
My branch, My splinter,
And I am Your tree.
Rest easy.
Let Me be Your cross, Your timber.
Rest easy on Me.

And the world will remember My Son,
My most precious One.
This Hill, This Hill
they call CALVARY.'

6:20 a.m., 27 July 1994

Come to Me, My Son,
And soon You will see
The race is won.
Come sit beside Me.

During that time of the trial,
I comforted You by saying,
'Let Me be that stone, that rock,
The grain in that cross,
That piece of timber.'

I was Your comforter.
They were both purely symbolic,
Both a very special feature.

For You are My branch,
And We are the tree.
I look at You at first glance.
Oh, how I love Thee.

And We will look upon this world
And see what they have learned.
My Son, You have excelled.
The destroyer is burned.

My Son, this world, these people
Will remember Thee
That cross, that timber, that tree,
That hill. Be still. That hill they called
CALVARY.

Father, here I am, nailed to this tree.
Satan's messengers of pain
Especially sent to Me.
Satan's tool of death
And severity of pain,
Though it will take My last breath,
Through this, I WILL GAIN.
And I will visit satan's home.
Through death's door, I will descend.
I will lecture him on his throne
And all of his men.

I will ascend to My Father,
AND YOU WILL SEE ME AGAIN
Sooner or later.
You'll know not when.

I will arrive with My saints and apostles,
My angels, yes, all of My men.
You will know MY MIGHT and MY GLORY
WHEN YOU SEE ME AGAIN!

And I will return peace and freedom to My people
And reclaim the land and the sea.
I will descend with My temple
Where I long to be.

For all time and in the future,
I hope My people understand and agree.
I hope they see
Why I died for their future
Nailed to this tree.

How I died for their sins,
Their sinful nature,
How I died for thee.
From now and forevermore,
I will never forget this war.
I will never forget this hill.
I will never forget this tree.
I will never forget this Hill they call CALVARY.

MY TABERNACLE

1:00 a.m., 28 July 1994

Tabernacle, Oh Tabernacle,
'Build' this for Me
Tabernacle, Oh Tabernacle,
For My Son and Me.

Somewhere to rest
Just for Me
A peaceful place
For My Son and Me.

A labyrinth of rooms
Somewhere to hide
Where My special people
I will see.
Through Me,
They will abide.

A labyrinth of rooms
A castle for Me
No longer a tent
On the desert sands But a special room
That looks so grand.

Somewhere for My spirit to rest You can see
A special home
For My Son and Me.

My people will do this for Me
A special home for My Son and Me
They will do this, you will see
For they will abide in Me.

Tabernacle, Oh Tabernacle,
You will see
That special home
For My Son and Me.

Oh, it will look so grand
That LIVING TREE
In that Special Home
For My Son and Me.

And My Son will descend.
With His Temple, you will see,
Especially built that SPECIAL BLEND,
Especially built for My Son and Me.

A labyrinth of rooms
ONE especially for Me,
A special room
Just for Me.

Tabernacle, Oh Tabernacle,
I long for this to be
Tabernacle, Oh Tabernacle,
Just forMe.

6:00 a.m

It has been thousands of years since I could see
That Tabernacle, that special tent you built for ME.
Across oceans of sand,
We roamed the land.
Until one day, you built Me a castle,
King Solomon's castle, just for Me.

Oh, it looked so grand
Amidst King Solomon's land
That special castle.
That Tabernacle Especially built for ME.

Oh, it has been so long since I was on My Earth.
Man, in the garden of Eden, We were robbed at birth.

All I want to see
Is My special House, My Home,
A place of indescribable and unrepeatable beauty,
And My Son especially adorned on His throne.

Oh Tabernacle, Oh Tabernacle,
My special House, My Place,
My Son's Throne, My Home.
I will reclaim this Earth in My grace.

And set up My Tabernacle,
My House, My Home,
My special castle
Especially for Jesus, His special throne,
His House, His Home.

Somewhere to rest, a special place
On Earth, there will be peace.
WE HAVE WON THE RACE.
In Heaven as on Earth, THY WILL BE DONE.
SOME DAY SOON YOU WILL SEE MY
KINGDOM COME.

That special place
That looks so Grand,
My special place
MY SPECIAL LAND.

12:05 p.m., 28 August 1994

Oh Tabernacle, Oh Tabernacle,
Build this for ME,
Especially for ME,
A castle built for THREE.

THE LIVING TREE

1:40 a.m., 2 August 1994

The Father says, I am the tree,
Two into the One.
I am the trunk.
My branch is My Son.

A person in the congregation
Saw the vision of a 'Tornado
Then a'Tree'
Followed by 'Peace' (A vision at St Peter's Church).

My Son and Me,
Soon We will come.
You will see.
We will bring you peace.
We will have won the race.
We will bring you peace.
We will bring Peace to this place.

For We are the Living Tree,
My Son and Me.
Yes, I am coming soon.
Soon you will see
This Living Tree,
My Son and Me.

PERSECUTION

4:00 a.m., 7 August 1994

Oh Persecution,
Execution,
You shoot me down in flames.
You have my sister and brother
Calling me all sorts of names.

You come to me.
You judge me.
When I have a job to do,
The Lord cries out in tears of blood and says,
'Oh, how I Love you.'

Sister and brother,
Do not judge one another
When we are all made of a different mould
But with the same clay.
If I may be so bold,
Listen to what I say.

If you can't comprehend another's work,
Don't cry foul and call it dirt
But understand the Lord is at work.
Do not persecute one another and hurt.
For we all have a special role to play.

Listen to what I say.
We are all from a different mould
But from the same clay.

For you must understand that when you
Persecute and hurt,
You are doing the enemy's work.
It just shows I am on the right track.
My Lord Jesus is with me
Both sides, front and back.
Oh, my King. Oh, I love Thee.

For I am Jesus, your King,
And you are a part of My ring.
I AM your Lord.
You are My sword.
Oh, how I love to hear thee sing.

You convey My message to My people.
From the heart of My steeple,
I AM with you both sides front and back.
My son, I Love you.
You ARE on the RIGHT TRACK.

Through My people,
The enemy shows his sleight of hand.
Satan persecutes within My steeple
And conflicts with your stand.

Yes, I am coming soon.

It will be so grand.

To the sound of trumpets and cymbals,

My special tune,

I Am Returning To Earth, My Special Land.

THE SUPER BEE

I AM the Super Bee.
Bring all that pollen to ME,
And I will give you spiritual honey.
Oh, how I long to set you free.

For you are all flowers
In My fields.
Your own special pollen
My family yields.

You feed ME your pollen.
You are raw and coarse.
I feed you your spiritual honey,
For I am your founder.
I am your source.

I put you all together
To make My special blend.
Soon I will send you My Special Messenger,
Jesus, My Son,
My beautiful, very special, and most HOLY ONE
And your very special friend.

Yes, I will give you spiritual honey.
I will give you peace and harmony.
My Son is coming soon you will see,
For He is coming to set you free.

MY KINGDOM

12:45 a.m., 18 August 1994

Thy Kingdom come,
Thy will be done
On Earth
As it is in Heaven.

To the sounds of trumpets and cymbals,
My special tune,
Soon you will see.
Yes, I am coming soon.

My trumpets pronounce.
My cymbals announce
The powers of My way.
Listen to what I say.
Yes, I am coming soon to stay.

AND NOBODY OR NOTHING WILL GET IN MY WAY!
For the Author is My trumpet.
He is My tool.
Have faith and believe in these words. It is your will.

He is one of My swords.
It is your will.
Think about these words and be still.

6:10 a.m., 18 August 1994

Yes, you are My trumpet,

A part of My special tune.

Our enemy's kingdom, I will crush it.

I am coming soon.

You will see.

You will see Me soon.

I am coming soon to set you free.

ETERNITY

3:10 a.m., 26 October 1994

Sister and Brother,
Turn to one another
And look into their eyes.

And say it is a beautiful day.
The Lord is coming back to stay.
What a beautiful surprise.

The Lord will show His radiant glow,
And you will know
Your own radiant glow,
For His river of life will flow.

He will loosen your chains
And set you free,
For He longs for you
To live His life for eternity.

For a thousand years, you will live this way.
And then one day,
The Lord will say,
'Would you like to live this way
For eternity, forever and a day?'

He will give you the choice,
And I'm sure you will rejoice.
The Lord will put you into gear,
For satan will be let loose that year.

The Lord is coming to set you free,
To live this way, this life for eternity,
And He will give you a new book of rules
Which will be like *The Family Jewels.*
Oh, how I long for this to be.

A SONG TO JESUS:
OUR WEDDING RING

8:20 p.m., 27 October 1994

Oh, Lord, how I want to see You.
Hear me sing
Praises and phrases
To You, Jesus, my King.

Oh, Lord, how I long to be Your bride
And a part of Your Ring
And to see You
For You to hear me sing

Praises and phrases
To You, Jesus,
My King.

Oh, Lord, tears come to my eyes.
That day will be such a beautiful surprise
As You show Yourself
When You come to this Earth.

For we will reach our hands to the sky
And sing
Praises and phrases
To You, Jesus,
Our king.

Oh, Lord, our Saviour,
Our Dragon Slayer,
Our Master of All Things,
We will look at You and adore You
And sing

Praises and phrases
To You, Jesus,
Our King,
Our beautiful Lord,
Our Majestic King.

I will walk amongst you all
And say this is a beautiful thing.
Oh, how I long to hear you sing to Me.

For you are My Ring.
You will sing
Praises and phrases,
For I am Jesus,
Your King.

3:00 a.m., 28 October 1994

We will all sing to Love
As I join with you
In this Ring.

I will join with you,
Singing to Love.
What a beautiful thing.

We will all join
In singing about each other's love.
We will sing
Praises and phrases
To this beautiful thing.

And, My friend, I love you and adore you
As we will sing
About the love of friendship and fellowship and mateship.
We will sing
Praises and phrases.
GOD created us with love.
What a beautiful thing.

And in the beginning
Was the WORD,
And the WORD was WITH GOD.

For I am Jesus, your Lord,
And I am HIS WORD.
I have judged you to be My sword,
For you are My Word.

This is a beautiful thing.
We will sing about GOD'S WORD.

We will sing
Praises in phrases
To Our Heavenly Father,
Our GOD and CREATOR,
And the Head of this Ring.

We will sing
Praises in phrases.
This is a beautiful thing.

Positive is the Word of the Lord,
A beautiful thing.
We will make up never-ending
Praises and phrases
To this beautiful thing.

3:40 a.m.

And WE will have a Covenant,
And on the left, we will have GOD THE FATHER
AND JESUS on our right
And in the middle will be US,
HIS RING.

And We will sing
Praises in phrases
To this beautiful thing,
Praises and phrases.
Oh, how I love to hear thee sing.

7:40 a.m.

Oh, WE will soon be coming for you ALL, My son,
And the Harvest will begin,
And the Loading will have begun.
And We will be singing
Praises in phrases
IN UNITY AS ONE.

8:15 a.m.

Praises in phrases
To JESUS,
Our most HOLY ONE.
We will sing praises in phrases
To Jesus, my King.

12:30 a.m., 31 October 1994

Praises in phrases
Of honour and glory
To the majesty Thy King.
Praises in phrases
To the glory of love,
What a beautiful thing.

Praises in phrases, My people will sing.
Praises in phrases, To the Glory
Thy Ring.

Praises in phrases,
What a beautiful thing.

To the Glory of GOD,
For He is our Rod.
To the children of God,
For we are His Rod.

To the Glory of power
And His majestic Ring.

To the Glory of Jesus,
For He is our King.

To the Light of Light,
To the PEACE He will bring.

We will sing to HIM
Praises in phrases.
We will sing
To our King.

We will sing praises in phrases
To the Elders of this Ring.
We will sing to the Glory of GOD.
What a beautiful thing.

To the Glory of Jesus,
OUR MAJESTIC KING.

To the Glory of love,
What a beautiful thing.

And We will sing to you,
GOD'S CHILDREN.
We will sing to the children
In this beautiful Ring.

We will sing about ANZACS.
Do you remember them sing
Of Waltzing Matilda
Or the Haka they did sing?

We will sing of their Spirit.
What an awesome thing.
We will Glorify them in love
In the Worldly Ring.

We will sing praises in phrases.
What an awesome thing.

We will sing to our King JESUS.
What a beautiful thing.
To the glory of our Saviour,
And this time, He did bring.
To our Heavenly Father,
Our GOD AND CREATOR,
And the Head of our Ring.

We will sing praises in phrases.
What a beautiful thing.

We will all sing
To each other.
We will sing of this
Beautiful event.

We will sing praises in phrases
To the wonder of this thing.
We will sing to GOD the FATHER
Who put us together
Into this beautiful thing.

We will sing of the warriors
Who fought for this beautiful thing
To the Glory of love.
To its Glory, we will sing.

To the Glory of MAN
And to GOD AND HIS WORD,
JESUS, our King,

Who created this Earth.
What a beautiful thing.

We will sing of this day.
We will sing of our future.
We will sing how we broke from our past.

From the Cocoon,
In eons of darkness,
We were captured by the enemy's thing.

And now we will sing to VICTORY,
To Man,
The Master of the Universe,

To the children of God,
The Father and Son,
The Head of our Ring.
What an awesome thing.

We will sing
Never-ending
Praises in phrases.

To the Glory of Love,
What an awesome thing.
What a beautiful sing.
What a beautiful thing.
What a beautiful Ring.

12:50 a.m. (EndMessage)

2:10a.m.

I will sing
Praises in phrases
To this Glorious thing.

I will sing to MAN
About OUR HEAVENLY FATHER, HIS SON JESUS,
AND HIS CHILDREN, THIS RING.

I will sing about this Battle
And the Glory it will bring.
I will sing about LOVE.
What a glorious and beautiful thing.

I will sing
To my FATHER,
My KING JESUS,
THE LEADERS OF THIS RING.

I will sing praises in phrases
To this Glorious Thing.

Praises in phrases
About our beautiful Ring,
This beautiful thing,
This Glorious RING,
This beautiful sing.

This gorgeous Ring,
This glamorous Ring,
This sparkling Ring,
This dazzling Ring.

To my LORD JESUS,
You Radiant King,
Your radiance You do bring
To Your beautiful RING.

Our Majestic KING,
To YOU, we do sing,
My beautiful KING.
This Glorious Ring,
This Glorious thing,
This Glorious sing,
This beautiful thing ...

NEVER-ENDING PRAISE TO YOU, LORD MOST HIGH.

LOVE AND GLORY

2:45 a.m., 31 October 1994

This is no time for pride.
I just take it in my stride.
I seek no glory.
I seek no fame.
I seek no record of my name.

For this, I do for Thee.
For this, I do for free.
I know You say
You shall reward me.

Then I say to Thee,
My Heavenly Father,
If You give me this fee,
I will use this reward
To further Your cause,
To help Thee,
For You are Thee.

I gladly do this for free
To please Thee,
For I so love Thee.

Andy, to you, I reward thee
For giving Me back this fee.
For this fee,
I now give back to thee.

For this, I give to you for free,
For I so love and adore thee.

For WE do this for each other,
WE do this for FREE.

For WE ALL so love one another,
For Love and Honour and Glory,
There is no fee.

For LOVE,
We always do this for free,
For WE all share the reward,
We share the fee.

We pass it round and round
As WE ALL share this GLORY.

AND ON TOP OF THIS MOUND
IS THE FATHER AND SON.
WHAT A BEAUTIFUL STORY,
WHAT BEAUTIFUL GLORY.

MY LOTION

6:30 p.m., 6 March 1996

To the Dolphins and Whales,
The mammals of the ocean,
I AM COMING SOON
TO SPREAD MY LOTION.

POSTSCRIPT

Depression leads to regression
And the forgiveness of sins.
Jesus Christ is with you and within
To forgive your sins.

Pray to the Holy Spirit,
And the Father will hear you.
Through His Son Jesus Christ,
He will steer you
Through forgiveness of sins.

Praise the Lord.

TELEPATHY

2:30 p.m., 26 October 1996

You, telepathic Lord, You,
You, shining great big sword, You,
You, shining gleaming sword, You,
You, beautiful Word, You.

For truth is My word, you,
Andy, hear of My truth
And tell others
I am coming back.
I will be back soon.

(Message received whilst listening 'Simply the Best' by Tina Turner
on the radio.)

TRUMPETS AND CYMBALS

4:30 a.m., 12 December 1996

People will try and discredit you
And conflict with your stand.
You will see the sounds of trumpets and cymbals.
They will be coming soon.
Oh, they will look so grand.

7:30 a.m., 17 December 1996

The trumpets and cymbals will pronounce
The comings of My way.
Listen to what I say.

10:30 a.m.

Yes, cymbals, God's cymbals,
The sounds of clashing, crashing thunder.
Watch out down under.
Nothing will get in My way!

11:30 a.m.

Yes, down under,
The enemy's throne will crumble and surrender
To the powers of My way.
This is the truth.
This is My word.
Listen to what I say.

The enemy's kingdom,
I will crush it
With the powers of My way.

My Kingdom come.
You will succumb to it.
Listen to what I say.

1:15 a.m., 18 December 1996

And death will be defeated
Under the power of My sting.
What a beautiful and wonderful thing.

Under God's blow,
What a Holy show,
Pure and bright,
A light of snow white.
Oh, what a Holy glow
We will show.

We have waited thousands of years,
So why not take all of the Glory?
Think of all the persecution, pain, and tears
This is a once only story.

Praise the Lord,
Glory to the Father,
Son and the Holy Spirit.

I AM COMING SOON

4:30 a.m., 19 December 1996

It was around 2,000 years ago
When Jesus made His name.
He lay in a manger
When He first came.

The three wise men came
To declare of His way.
Andy, you're a man Heavenly guided
To declare what I say.

I spent 33 years on My Earth
To declare what I say.
Heavenly-sent from birth,
Listen to what I say.

I came to save My people
To take away their sins.
I longed to be in My Temple.
A new stage begins.

And I will be coming back
This second time, with fire in My eyes,
With thunder and lightning, that certain crack.
It is the enemy I despise.

And people will be separated
The weeds from the grain.
And all those who are with Me,
They will forever gain.

I am the way, the truth, and the life,
Before I come back, there will be much strife.
And the river of life will flow.
There will be many reborn
With a Heavenly-sent glow.

And you will praise Me forever and ever.
Because of this Earthly historic show,
My Universe will know of this Earth.
From afar, it will see its Heavenly-sent glow.

And My Universe will know this Earth
And its Heavenly-sent glow.
I will show My Universe Peace and Harmony
And how to be still.
This is My natural-born WILL.

Through My Earth as My Kingdom comes,
This Earth will grow from My rebirth.
It is God's natural roll
To expand His Universe with His people
And to stroll and stroll and stroll.

And God's Children will inherit this Earth.
This is His will
To the Universe, Peace, and Harmony
And how to be still.

God's promise came to Earth –
All the colours of the rainbow.
You are about to go through a natural rebirth
And be reborn with a wonderful,
Beautiful, Holy, natural GLOW!

And God will reclaim His Earth.
His plans are unfolding
To give His children their inheritance,
Their natural rebirth.
My children will be at peace on Earth,
Strolling, strolling, strolling.

And this Universe will know My Earth.
This is My natural laid-out Will
To show My Universe peace and harmony
And how to be still.

And Man will stand out brave and strong,
His arms outstretched,
His legs firm, strong and long,
His Woman at his side.
Through Me, you will all Abide.

I have waited eons of years.
My plans are unfolding.
You have no idea about My Heavenly Tears.
My plans are unrolling.

And it is not long to go.
Do you remember My promise with the Rainbow?
And soon I will sit back with a Heavenly-sent sigh
As I look upon this all happening.
It is most beautiful to My Eye,
This Heavenly-sent chastening.

Yes, you will all kneel and tremble
When I arrive.
Soon you will see My Heavenly-sent Temple.
Through Me, you Will Abide.

And every knee shall bow,
And every tongue confess.
For in His Hand will be His Love,
And out of His mouth a mighty two-edged sword.

He has many beautiful plans for those
Whom, through Him, they did abide.
He will give the World His Glory,
And you will take it in your stride.

So many beautiful plans for this Earth,
So much Peace and Harmony.
Oh, it will look so beautiful,
God's present to you, your rebirth,
So very, very lovely.

Yes, My Earth will know this rebirth.
This is truly, truly happening,
And Jesus will destroy all death
And show His gird and girth.
The Groom and Bride long for their promised
Wedding Ring.
A Ding-a-ling-a-ling.

Hallelujah, Hallelujah, Hallelujah!
Praise the Lord, Praise the Lord, Praise the Lord.

BE PREPARED

For all those non-Christian religions,
Please read the New King James Version Bible
And read the story of the Tower of Babel
And how I made you all babble, babble, babble.

For the time is coming.
It is very short
To turn from your ways.
This is no game. This is no sport.
Please turn from your ways.

I am coming soon
As sure as Earth has a Moon.
Please listen to what I say,
For I am Jesus, I am your Lord.
Please, you will turn to My Way.

This is no joke.
This is no hoax.
The power of My Ways.

I LOVE ALL the people of My Earth.
However, I have a very special role
To all those Christians who stood by Me
From My Birth.

This could be assumed
As a warning
From one of My people.
I have a very special role.
Wait until you see My Temple
I long to be with you all
And stroll and stroll and stroll.

12:45

You have had 2,000 years
From My Birth.
Through Me, you could aspire.
My Bible has been sent
Throughout the Earth.
It is loyalty I admire.

Please take this as a warning,
All the peoples of Earth.
It is not too late to turn to Me.
It is to freedom I aspire.

Please believe that I am your Lord
From the beginning of time.
I admire other religious causes,
But it is to Me you must aspire.

I love you all,
All the peoples of My Earth.
It will be your Heavenly-sent Glow,
For you are all relatives since God gave birth.
Surely, this you must know.

So the time is becoming very short
To make your decision.
Either you believe in God the Father
And His Son, Jesus Christ your Lord,
Or you will be in for an incision.

I don't know how to say it more plainly.
This will be your will.
Either believe in Me, your Lord Jesus Christ,
And your Heavenly Father,
The Creator of all things,
Better for you sooner than later,
And show this Earth how to be still.

This Author is My Trumpet.
He does not make this up at will.
Christians do not lie.
They long for this Earth to be at peace and to be
Still.

And as for death, it will die,
Yes, as for death, I will sever it.
I do not lie.
Yes, you will praise Me forever and ever and ever,
And initially, you will CRY.

1:30 a.m.

Andy is an Aussie,
And he is concerned.

He has been through many Asian countries.
Please, for you, this you must discern.

He made many friends with you.
He travelled twice through many places of My World.
He loves All peoples of this Earth.
His love for you he still holds as he has held.
He has been to Bali
And to Java,
Singapore and Bangkok,
And he has loved you all.

Please remember My message in My Bible.
Love Thy Neighbour.
Please believe in Me. Believe in these words
And turn to My Bible.
Don't you understand that it is only just purely, simply tribal?

For Australians are some of My people,
And Andy is crying.
They love this Earth, they are only a few,
But through them, I'm aspiring.

Yes, Andy has been to
Lebanon, North Africa, Europe, Canada, and the USA.
He has spoken to people with different beliefs
And listened to what they say.

He has found we all have one thing in common –
The love of people.

I have seen them through his eyes.
Wait till you see My Temple.

Yes, I know you all.
You are all one of a kind,
But you must read My Bible.
Please turn to Me before it is too late
And forget it is just purely, simply tribal.

Yes, this is the most historic
Important message to you all.
These writings are not just symbolic
But an Almighty, God-Fearing, Historical Call.
So please, may I plead with you
And say once again,
This is not a Christian war cry,
But it is from Me, Jesus, your Lord and friend.

Please lay down your weapons
And live in harmony.
Please look to those around you
And feed the Hungry.

It is most important that you look inside yourselves
And realise that satan caused the sin of death.
He hates you ALL.
He causes wars, famine, diseases, and your last breath.
All he wants you to do is to make you crawl.

Yes, satan is My enemy,
And for him, I have vengeance in store.
And all those who are with him,
You will know terror for evermore.

Don't let satan convert you
Or make you conflict with your stand.
Know no fear and turn to Me,
And I will lend you My Hand.

You must understand
This is a once-only offer.
The prizes I have in store for you are very, very grand.
Please turn to those friends you Love, your Sister and Brother.
And make this your final, last stand.

Yes, it is most important that you fight satan's will,
Especially those non-Christians.
Please turn to US,
And I your Lord will help you beat the enemy
And give you peace and show you how to be still.
Yes, Peace on Earth,
This will be very, very lovely.

Yes, these are important words,
An Historical Event.
It will be much sooner than later
That this Earth will become Heavenly-sent.

Yes, Thy Kingdom Come On Earth,
As It Is In Heaven.
You are all about to go through a rebirth.
God's Holy number for love is '7'.

Yes, in My hand, there are Seven Stars,
And in My mouth a two-edged sword.
I don't know why you want to travel to Mars
When soon you will know Me, for I am Your Lord.

7:00 a.m.

Now you are all different tribes on Earth –
A Babble, babble, babble.
But when you simply think about it,
Now you are all one tribe on one Earth.
Now please read My Bible.

Now I Am Coming Soon,
So please forget that you are all differently tribal
And realize that I AM THE SON OF MAN.
Please read about Me in your Bible.

You must realize that you are all relatives
From the beginning of time.
God made you all in His Image
And called you MANKIND.

Yes, MAN KIND.
Don't you realize what this is saying?
To be kind to each other and nurture each other,
And yes, to God the Father, Son, and Holy Spirit,
You must be praying.

Please remember your spiritual teachings on this Earth –
To Love All of Creation
And to live in Peace and Harmony.
You are All about to go through a rebirth,
Every single nation.

I don't know how to say this more plainly.
I don't want you to go to war.
Just turn to your Sister and Brother
And say 'the Lord is coming back.
I think we should turn to Him before . ..'

Yes, so many parties and prizes
And fireworks galore.
You have no idea of the plans for all of you,
The things I have in store.

PRAISE THE LORD.
GLORY TO THE FATHER,
SON, AND THE HOLY SPIRIT
FOREVER MORE.

A MESSAGE FROM JESUS

4:40 p.m., 6 February 1997

Yes, there are special musical themes on the radio
That blends in with your thinking.
Don't forget we are in a Spiritual war.
Don't listen to satan's music,
For it is through him you will be sinking.

4:50 p.m.

Now the time is becoming short
To publish these poems, Andy.
This is no sport.
You have been very, very handy.

Yes, I know you are shy,
And for this, I will give you privacy.
Soon you will see ME in the sky,
And to ME, it will be PURELY, SIMPLY,
LOVELY!

I'LL CATCH YOU LATER

8:20 p.m., 23 February 1997

Yes, I may come back in your lifetime.
Then again, I may not.
I will do this in My Father's time.
Are you ready or not?

I'll catch you later.
My Father is the instigator,
And I am His Son.

Satan is the berator.
I'll catch you later,
And there will be fun in the sun
For those allotted ones.

For I am Jesus, His Son,
A most Holy One.
Yes, fun with the Son
For those allotted ones.

THAT INTERNAL VOICE

12:20 a.m., 14 April 1998

You hear this internal voice.
To you, He is saying,
'Have faith and rejoice,
For I am all-knowing.'

Yes, this beautiful voice
You are receiving,
A guiding light of heavenly force,
Oh yes, and of course, it's all-knowing.

You have the choice
To listen to My Word,
Oh yes, and to rejoice
At My two-edged sword.

For Heaven and Earth
Will be at peace again,
A heavenly rebirth
From whence it began.

Yes, the Seventh Seal,
It is to be opened
With no appeal
To the very end.

For the SON OF MAN
Will be riding His white horse.
The Heavenly gate will open.
There will be no remorse.

For this is something that has to be done.
The play is unfolding.
This war will be won.

Yes, the Son of Man will be seen
By all here on Earth.
His promised return will soon begin,
Giving us a spiritual rebirth.

Yes, a spiritual awareness
To all at hand.
Yes, a natural progression
As Christians show their stand.

For the time is coming
When every tongue shall confess.
Jesus is Lord.
On our knees, we shall redress.

For peace and spiritual harmony
Will be at hand.
As the lion lies down with the sheep and the child,
There will be peace over our land.

Yes, that internal voice will not die.
You are not going crazy. This is no lie,
For too many Christians have heard this same voice.
It is up to you to accept it or reject it. That is your choice.

Spiritual harmony is at hand.
The war is unfolding over this land.
The end times are here. Let's make a stand.
After all, this is God's Earth
Our inheritance, His land
Since Adam and Eve's birth,
Once a Holy Land.

Yes, do not love money,
But ask for prosperity,
And I will pour on you your spiritual honey,
Which is purely, simply, lovely.

Yes, accept My laws,
And I will chastise, yes, instruct you.
Open up your doors,
And I will hear from above you.

Yes, pray to Me in tongues
Or however you feel comfortable,
And I will be like a sponge.
Listening to you will be most wonderful.

For I love it when you pray to Me.
On every word, I rejoice.
For I love you all, don't you see?
Have faith and accept Me. That is your choice.

Yes, faith can move mountains.
It is a wonderful thing.
Soon it will be curtains,
For the enemy will know My sting.

Yes, satan is in for a shock
When I return.
Yes, for My heavenly flock
Will watch him burn.

Oh yes, did I tell you about My heavenly voice?
It will one day come inside all of you.
Surely you must rejoice,
For it is from Me, far above you.

Yes, you have free will
To accept or reject Me.
Sit quietly and be still.
Let Me give you your fill
And plant the seed in you and see!

A MESSAGE FROM
FATHER GOD

3:30 a.m., 29 October 1994

I have put My food on this dish and handed
it out to you all on a plate.
Will you receive from Andrew about My Word?
Will you read My Bible, My Word? Read this book.

The story of My Son. Read of the beginnings of
Everyone – of The Human Race.

Soon you will be face-to-face with My Son. Read this book.
The Bible. My Book. I have handed it to you on a plate.

9:45 p.m., 7 March 1996

John 1:1,2
In the beginning was the Word, and the Word
was with God, and the Word was God.
He was in the beginning with God.
(New King James Version: Spirit-Filled Life Bible)

6:30 p.m., 8 March 1996

John 1:14
And the Word became flesh and dwelt among us, and we beheld
His glory, the glory as of the only begotten of the Father, full of
grace and truth.
(New King James Version: Spirit-filled Life Bible)
Jesus is the Word. Turn to the Lord.

9:45 p.m., 2 March 2007

Now a Dying Planet. Soon to become a Life Planet.

5:20 p.m., 16 April 07

KEEP THE FAITH.
LOVE OVERCOMES ALL–
PURE LOVE.

7:00 p.m., 12 January 2010

The Lord says, 'I AM GOING TO TAKE AWAY THE SUFFERING.'

Revelation 21:4
And God will 'wipe away every tear from there eyes; there shall be
no more death, nor sorrow, nor crying. There shall be no more pain,
for the former things have passed away."

5:30 p.m., 18 March 2024

Jerusalem, wait until you see my temple,
for my temple is beautiful
(so sayeth the Lord Jesus)

5:20 p.m., 5 September 2024

The Holy Spirit will leave
the earth within Gods people.
And be united with God in heaven,
before returning to the earth
to establish Gods kingdom.

Peace be with you my children.
You will meet the Lord in the sky.
if you are a believer

Thessalonians 1.4.17.

Thy Kingdom come Thy will be done on Earth as it is in Heaven

AUTHOR'S NOTE

My love to you, dear reader, my sister, my brother, peace be with you.

The Lord is bringing harmony to Earth. Keep the faith. He is coming soon. We are on call. It is only right and logical that He comes now to guide us as we journey out from the planet. The Lord Jesus is coming to show us the way, the truth, and the light of life.

Thy Kingdom come, Thy will be done, on Earth as it is in Heaven.

Please be tolerant of all people, for the world is full of characters, each with a special talent and a different role to play. Please try not to indulge in snobbery or to judge yourselves as better than another. Please try not to consider a person's physical, monetary, intellectual, or spiritual standing, for we are all born equal in the eyes of God, with much to learn and much to give. Remember that we are all of a different mould but from the same clay. Remember how it says in the Bible: faith, hope, charity, and above all, love.

Consider the non-believers, for they especially need our guidance. Do not be frustrated if you cannot enlighten them, for all you can do is plant the seed. Remember, a crop will never grow unless you plant the seed. Ask them to pray. The Holy Spirit will bring them awareness when their time comes. Expect persecution, for it is the enemy's way. Please try not to sin, for it cracks the foundation between God and yourself. Repent and pray to the Lord Jesus, for He will repair those cracks and rid that burden.

Paradise is coming to Earth. Peace on Earth and goodwill to all people of the Earth. The Lord Jesus is bringing peace to Earth.

Have you seen the dawn lately? The sunrise? Please take a look. Well, human history is about to go through a giant leap. The dark ages are about to end. We are in the dawning of humanity, and soon we will see the Son. Goodbye to the night sky. Here comes the light. The grace of the Lord will soon be here.

Remember, Jesus is Lord.

Peace be with you.

Andrew Hector (A Retired House Painter)

PS: Remember how it says in the Bible, 'The day of the Lord will come like a thief in the night' THIS IS SHORT NOTICE.

AND ALL THE BELIEVERS WILL BE RAPTURED UP.

AND THERE WILL BE A NEW HEAVEN AND A NEW EARTH.
(Revelation 21:1)

REMEMBER THE BIBLE SAYS THERE IS LITTLE OR NO NOTICE.
FOR THE LOVE OF MANKIND AND TO GOD BE THE GLORY!

THE SOUTHERN CROSS
GOD BLESS YOU

7:00 p.m., 11 March 2010

 THORNS

 NAIL

 NAIL

 SPEAR

NAIL

IN THE UNIVERSE FOR ALL TO SEE FOR YOU AND ME

CRITIQUE

Andy,

You gave me your Praises in Phrases to
read and to offer any comment.

Firstly, let me say how honoured I feel to be
given this material. It is a very special part of
your personal life during a period when you
chose to be attentive to the voice of the Lord.

Your writings are a combination of your life
experiences along with the exciting aspects of God's
responses which are so evident in 'A Song To Jesus',
'Our Wedding Ring', and 'Love and Glory'. We are
all human souls who, from time to time, cry out to
our Maker. Our God is always wanting us to listen to
Him, but so often, we are too busy or not willing.

You have said yes to the Lord, and the Spirit has
given you the words to write. In your Preface, you
say, 'The Lord has asked me to publish these poems.'
Maybe it is time you did something about it.

It is a wonderful experience reading words
that have been inspired by the Spirit of God.
Hence, the Bible can be read over and over and
each time we can hear God speaking to us.

In 'Quantum Leap' you wrote,
'His Universe beckons us
To sow His seed.'

Surely then our role is the same as that given
to the disciples – 'Go ye therefore and teach
all nations.' You wrote in 'The Tap', 'You
are my tool, my warrior, my word.'

How intimate is the voice of the Lord when He
says in 'A Code in the Night', 'I have put you on a
path of discovery. I'll lead you to a full recovery.'

I particularly liked the word pictures in 'Loneliness'.
You certainly have a depth of understanding
of how loneliness affects us and how it also
affected Jesus. It is a piece that is not just about
abandonment; you express a positive aspect as well:

'A time of self-confidence
A time to make a stand
This is my incidence.
There must be a lesson at hand.'

'Pain' is a highly descriptive short piece that enables
the reader to understand how easy severe pain
can lead to thoughts of suicide. You are clear in
stating how this action needs to be overcome and
the devil cheated of his prize. I enjoyed the analogy
of the 'dartboard numbered with names'.

'Psych Ward' was born out of what was obviously a powerful phase of your life. You have a strong understanding of how our God can be present, even in those who have been locked away from humanity. 'And the dominoes started to fall as everybody started to change."

The Holy Spirit, depicted by your 'dove of peace', was there for you, and you realised your importance even as 'a child, a humble servant'.

The poems 'I am', 'A Promise', 'Eternity', and 'I Am Coming Soon' contain groups of statements explaining how Jesus will come again:

'I am coming soon. I do not lie. I am Me. I am coming soon to set you free.'

These contain exciting verses that talk of heaven and God's love, of what is and what will be. I sometimes get concerned that some people attempt to frighten others into fearing the Second Coming. If we truly believe in the promise of Christ, we should be looking forward to the event.

In 'Calvary', you showed you have a deep meaningful understanding of the way of the Cross. It is a piece that shows much feeling and love towards a saviour crucified.

'Persecution' is a poem that explains how important it is not to be judgemental towards one another but to accept we are all made from the same 'clay' but in different 'moulds'. I particularly liked,

'If you can't comprehend another's work,
Don't cry foul and call it dirt.'

'A Message from Jesus' shows how we can hear Him talking to us in so many different ways. The lyrics from songs heard on the radio can easily blend in with a message Jesus has for us. Often music can also be a trigger and support His words.

I used this concept extensively in my Christian radio programming to support my little stories about life which always had a thought at the end that tied in with the overall message and the backing music.

There is no doubt you listened when you heard 'That Internal Voice':

'You hear this internal voice.
To you, He is saying, "Have faith and rejoice."'

Congratulations, Andy. I can only encourage you to keep listening to what the Lord has to say to you and keep writing. The world needs to hear the Lord's message, and you are a messenger.

Find a way to get your material onto the World Wide Web and then pray to the Holy Spirit that those who need to read your messages will be led to your website.

From 'Be Prepared',

'Andy is an Aussie, And he is concerned.'

Keep being concerned, Andy. Keep the faith and turn each day into a prayer of thanks.

Peter Mack, 4 August 2003 ('Stories about Life' can be found on Peter's

website www.thatslife.cc.)

AUTHOR'S NOTE

You pray to the Father, Son, and Holy Spirit
Because it is mutual love.

The Holy Trinity loves you.
One God now and forever.
Amen.

The Holy Trinity:
Father God, Lord God, and the Holy Spirit.

You pray to God for many reasons.
Let me count the ways!
There is No End.

THE GRACE OF THE FATHER, SON AND THE HOLY
SPIRIT BE WITH YOU ALL.
GOD'S GRACE,
AMAZING GRACE.
TO GOD BE THE GLORY!